L I F E V I E W S

Published by Creative Education
123 South Broad Street, Mankato, Minnesota 56001
Creative Education is an imprint of The Creative Company

Art direction by Rita Marshall; Production design by The Design Lab

Photographs by Galyn C. Hammond, JLM Visuals (Burton A. Amundson, Charlie Crangle, Robert Greenler,
Ken & Helga Heiman, Richard P. Jacobs, Breck P. Kent, John Minnich, Mike Reblin), Robert McCaw,
Eugene G. Schulz, Tom Stack & Associates (Terry Donnelly, Jeff Foott, Sharon Gerig, Barbara Gerlach, Thomas
Kitchin, Joe McDonald, Allen B. Smith, Doug Sokell, Spencer Swanger), Unicorn Stock Photos (Robert E. Barber)

Library of Congress Cataloging-in-Publication Data

George, Michael.
Glaciers / by Michael George.
p. cm. — (LifeViews)
ISBN 1-58341-253-0
1. Glaciers—Juvenile literature. I. Title. II. Series.
GB2403.8 .G53   2003
551.31'2—dc21   2002034786

First Edition

2 4 6 8 9 7 5 3 1

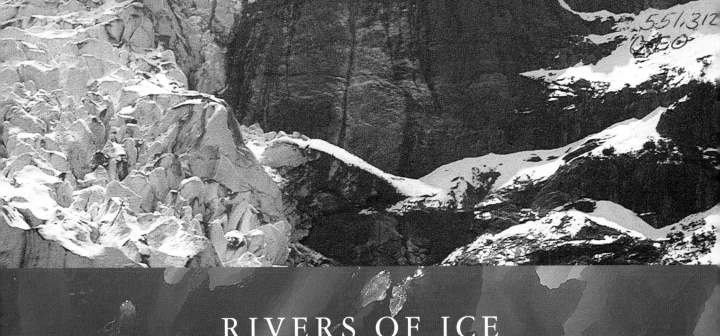

RIVERS OF ICE
GLACIERS

MICHAEL GEORGE

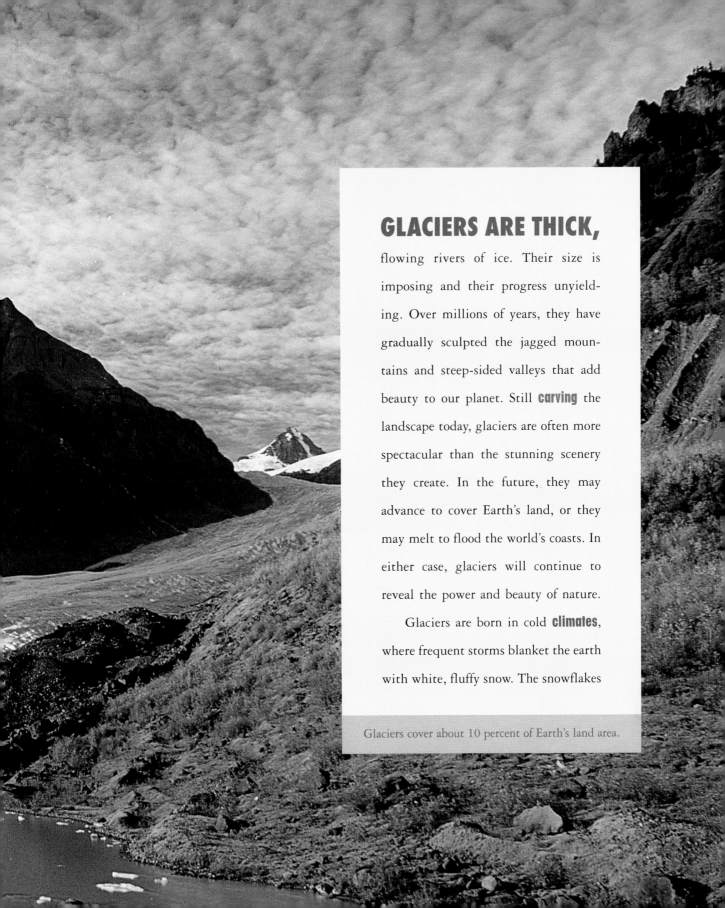

GLACIERS ARE THICK,

flowing rivers of ice. Their size is imposing and their progress unyielding. Over millions of years, they have gradually sculpted the jagged mountains and steep-sided valleys that add beauty to our planet. Still **carving** the landscape today, glaciers are often more spectacular than the stunning scenery they create. In the future, they may advance to cover Earth's land, or they may melt to flood the world's coasts. In either case, glaciers will continue to reveal the power and beauty of nature.

Glaciers are born in cold **climates**, where frequent storms blanket the earth with white, fluffy snow. The snowflakes

Glaciers cover about 10 percent of Earth's land area.

that cover the ground come in a variety of forms, including icy needles, dusty powder, and six-sided **crystals**. After a time, snowflakes on the ground lose their lacy shapes and join together into tiny balls of ice. These grains of ice can be seen in dirty snowdrifts, or on the side of the road on a spring day.

As the days of spring grow gradually warmer, the sun's rays melt Earth's blanket of snow. In some areas, however, temperatures never rise high enough to melt the grains of snow. In **polar** regions and atop high mountains, fresh snow piles up year after year, burying older grains of snow under a thick, heavy layer of insulation. The tremendous weight compresses the grains of snow, and they fuse together. Eventually, pockets of air that surround the grains are even forced out. What was once a covering of soft, white snow becomes a slab of hard, blue ice.

As the years pass, snow continues to accumulate and the slab of ice grows steadily thicker. Eventually, the slab

A glacier's thickness is about one-half of its surface width. Small glaciers may be anywhere from 30 to 300 feet (10–90 m) thick, while large Alaskan glaciers may measure nearly a mile (1.6 km) or more.

becomes too massive to sit peacefully still. Just as gravity pulls a skier down a ski slope, gravity pulls the ice down the mountain. Once the ice begins to move, it is called a glacier.

A glacier follows the path of existing valleys like a slow-flowing river of ice. The **speed** at which a glacier moves depends on the thickness of the ice and on the steepness of the slope. The fastest glaciers are hundreds of feet thick and flow down steep mountains. Temperature also affects a glacier's speed. Glaciers move most quickly when temperatures are warm because they slide on a thin, slippery layer of water. The **distance** that most glaciers move in a day ranges from several inches to several feet. However, the fastest glaciers cover more than 100 feet (30 m) a day.

Surprisingly, all parts of a glacier do not move at the same speed. This fact is easily observed by placing stakes across the width of a glacier. After a time, the stakes in the middle are farther downhill than those near the edges, revealing that the middle of a glacier moves faster than its edges. A glacier's various layers also move at different speeds. Metal pipes drilled

Norway's Svartison Glacier (opposite) moves at an average glacial pace. The record for fastest glacial surge belongs to the Kutiah Glacier in Pakistan. It once moved more than seven miles (12 km) in three months.

deep into glaciers eventually bend, showing that the surface moves faster than deeper layers. This is because the layers of ice nearest the earth are slowed by the underlying terrain.

On its journey down a mountain, a glacier encounters a variety of obstacles. Few things, however, can stop a glacier's progress. When a glacier encounters a sharp corner or bend, the brittle ice cracks with loud, piercing snaps. The resulting fissures, called **crevasses**, can be hundreds of feet deep and tens of feet wide. Crevasses usually appear as parallel gouges in the glacier's surface. Sometimes crevasses intersect and form towering pinnacles of ice called séracs.

As a glacier weaves its way downhill, the ice flows over underlying rocks. Ice has an adhesive grip, which you can feel if you touch a cold ice cube tray with damp hands. Because of this grip, rocks stick to glaciers and give the ice tremendous powers of **erosion**. Like a giant file, the flowing rocks and ice grate the underlying terrain. Atop high peaks, where glaciers are born and nourished with falling snow, the glacial ice gouges mountainsides into bowl-shaped hollows

Temperate glaciers, found where the winters average above 32 °F (0 °C) and the summers above 50 °F (10 °C), accumulate the most snow. They also melt the most, allowing them to pick up vast amounts of erosive materials.

called cirques. When two glaciers occupy valleys that lie side by side, they produce a sharp, jagged ridge known as an arête. Occasionally, a mountain peak is completely surrounded by glaciers. Over many years, the glaciers eat into the mountain, carving the peak into a pointed, pyramid-shaped horn.

Farther down the mountain, a glacier plows through rock, **soil**, and vegetation like a gigantic bulldozer, carving the V-shaped valleys cut by rivers into steep-sided, U-shaped troughs. The material scraped from the earth dirties the clean, white surface of the glacier. Most of this rocky **debris** is pushed aside and piles up along the edges of the glacier. The rest is carried all the way to the glacier's base, where it is finally dumped. The resulting pile of material, called a moraine, contains rock and soil in a variety of forms: from unworn, massive boulders to finely grated silt.

Glaciers are awesome instruments of erosion, relentlessly plowing through the earth and its vegetation. A glacier's forward progress, however, can be stopped by two equally

Glaciers create valleys and fiords by erosion (wearing material from Earth's surface), but they create landforms such as moraines by deposition (laying matter down). Erratic boulders (left) are rocks carried far from their source by glaciers.

mighty forces. One of these is **heat**. When the bone-chilling days of winter are replaced by the mild days of spring, warm winds and sunshine soften the surface of the glacier. The glacier glistens with moisture as streams of **meltwater** wear channels, tunnels, and caves in the ice.

Although the glacier continues to flow downhill, warm temperatures completely melt the flowing ice at its base. As a result, the glacier may actually stop its forward progress, or even melt backward up the mountain. Eventually, the base stops its retreat where summer temperatures remain below freezing. Here the glacier waits for winter, when cold temperatures allow it to advance once again.

In some regions, summer temperatures are not warm enough to stop a glacier's forward progress. Instead, perpetually cold temperatures enable the rivers of ice to flow all the way to the ocean. The sea, however, is as potent an adversary as the warm summer sun; it is the second mighty force that can halt a glacier. Wherever glaciers meet the coast, enormous **ice shelves** extend over the water, towering hundreds

Valley glaciers often carry large amounts of rock debris. When they reach the sea or a lake, they break off in chunks and form icebergs, which slowly release the debris into the water as they melt.

of feet above the surface. Waves smash against the ice, caus-
ing massive chunks to break off and crash into the ocean.
This process is called calving, and the masses of ice that float
out to sea are called **icebergs**. Once freed from land, icebergs
float toward warmer climates. Gradually, the sun's rays melt
the islands of ice.

Polar seas, such as the North Atlantic, are often littered
with thousands of icebergs. These icebergs are calved from
ice sheets, enormous layers of ice and snow that have completely buried polar land masses. With only the sea to stop
their spread, ice sheets produce most of the world's icebergs.

There are only two ice sheets on Earth's surface: one in
Antarctica and the other in Greenland. The Greenland ice
sheet covers 670,000 square miles (1.7 million sq km) and is
almost two miles (3.2 km) thick at its center. Many times
larger than the Greenland ice sheet, the Antarctic ice sheet
covers more than five million square miles (13 million sq
km)—an area larger than the United States, Mexico, and
Central America put together. Two and a half miles (4 km)

Icebergs calved from ice shelves are some of the largest. One iceberg, called
B-9, calved from an Antarctic ice shelf, measured nearly twice the size of Rhode
Island! It eventually broke into smaller icebergs.

thick at its center, the Antarctic ice sheet hides entire mountain ranges beneath its surface. This enormous layer of ice accounts for 90 percent of all the ice in the world and contains more water than all of Earth's rivers and lakes combined.

Although the Greenland and Antarctic ice sheets seem enormous, they are small when compared to the ice sheets that existed long ago. Thousands of years ago, Earth's climate was cooler than it is today, and ice sheets covered much of the land. In fact, ice sheets have advanced several times in Earth's history. Each period of ice advance, called an **ice age** or a glacial epoch, is followed by a period when temperatures warm and the ice retreats to the cold polar regions of the globe. The warm climate we enjoy today caused the latest retreat of the ice sheets.

Although 12,000 years have passed since the last ice age, ancient glaciers left lasting imprints on Earth's surface, just as modern glaciers do today. Ancient glaciers are responsible for the cirques, arêtes, and U-shaped valleys that decorate many mountainsides. Small valleys often hang high above the floor

Glaciers leave behind many clues about where they've been. U-shaped valleys, cirques, scraped rock, and erratic boulders are all indicators. During the last ice age, glaciers covered more than 30 percent of Earth's land area.

of the largest U-shaped valleys. These hanging valleys were carved by small tributary glaciers that combined with larger, more powerful glaciers.

There is also evidence of past ice ages on level land. As the glaciers advanced, finely ground silt polished smooth the underlying **bedrock**. At the same time, jagged rocks stuck in the ice gouged deep scratches across the smoothened bedrock. In northern regions these scrapes can still be seen, along with the rounded boulders and moraines that the glaciers deposited.

Ancient glaciers are also responsible for the stunning scenery along some coasts. During past glacial periods, the enormous ice sheets that covered the globe tied up much of Earth's water. As a result, **sea levels** were much lower than they are today. Naturally, glaciers descended to the former sea level, carving their characteristic steep-sided valleys. As the climate warmed, the ice sheets melted and sea levels rose, filling the valleys with water. Today, these submerged valleys, called fiords, indent the coasts of many regions. The

Glaciers continually shape the earth. Moraines and erratic boulders dot the land. Melting ice creates cascading waterfalls. Advancing and retreating glaciers polish surface rock and carve magnificent valleys and fiords.

most spectacular fiords are found along the coast of Norway.

Earth's landscape reveals abundant evidence of past ice ages. Only recently, however, did scientists come up with an adequate explanation for past glacial periods. Most scientists now believe that ice ages are caused by variations in Earth's **orbit** around the sun. Periodically, Earth moves farther from the sun. As a result, the amount of heat we receive from the sun decreases, Earth's climate cools, and the ice sheets advance.

In the past, periods of warmer climate and retreating ice have lasted about 10,000 years. Since the current period of retreating ice has already lasted 12,000 years, some scientists believe another period of glaciation is long overdue. However, human activities may postpone this expected ice age. When we destroy forests and burn **fossil fuels**, we increase the amount of carbon dioxide in the atmosphere. The additional carbon dioxide traps the sun's heat, much like a blanket. Therefore, instead of a gradual cooling, there may be a gradual warming of Earth's climate.

The scientific study of glaciers—how they form, move, grow, and affect life on Earth—is called glaciology. A person who studies glaciers is a glaciologist.

Although a warmer climate seems preferable, it may not necessarily be better than a colder one. Significantly warmer temperatures could melt much of the world's ice, and the results might be disastrous. If the world's glaciers and ice sheets melted, sea levels would rise more than 200 feet (61 m) and flood vast areas of the planet. Cities such as London and Paris would be underwater, along with entire countries, such as Denmark and the Netherlands.

Whether the glaciers retreat or advance, human civilization and the world **environment** are intimately related to these relentless rivers of ice. Although they are formed by delicate snowflakes, glaciers grow to imposing sizes, and build awesome strength. They challenge the bravest explorers, sculpt jagged mountain peaks, and carve coastal fiords. Whether they flood the world with water or cover the land with ice, glaciers embody the power and beauty of nature.

Even granite eventually yields to a glacier's power.

A MODEL GLACIER

Like massive bulldozers, glaciers carve the earth's surface into some of the most spectacular landscapes imaginable. This model will show you on a very small scale how glaciers sculpt the land over which they travel.

You Will Need

- A sandbox
- Water
- Several small rocks and pebbles
- Plaster of Paris
- Measuring cups
- A mixing bowl
- A mixing spoon

Building the Glacier

1. Wet the sand and scoop out a hole in the shape of a half-circle, about two to three inches (5–8 cm) deep and at least a foot (30 cm) wide and long, with sloping sides.

2. Scatter a few rocks and pebbles across the floor of the depression.

3. Shape a snakelike sand ridge about one inch (3 cm) high from the flat edge of the depression to the opposite edge.

4. Mix a batch of plaster of Paris to the consistency of thin pudding and carefully pour it into the depression, filling it to the top.

5. Before the plaster sets, press a few pebbles into the top. Sprinkle with sand.

6. Once your model has hardened, remove it from its bed.

Observation

Prepare a smooth sand bed, then set the "glacier" on it. Slowly push down and forward, the curved edge leading the way. Notice the marks left behind. Because of the adhesive property of ice, glaciers pick up rocks and drag them across the earth's surface as they move. These rocks (like those embedded in the bottom of your model) grate the underlying terrain, carving hollows and valleys.

The winding ridge of sand left by your model is called an esker (ES-kur). Eskers indicate that meltwater streams once tunneled through or under the glacial ice. The esker itself is a ridge of debris deposited by the stream when it stopped flowing.

As you move the model, notice how sand piles up along its sides and leading edge. In nature, boulders, gravel, sand, and clay are carried along with the glacier as it moves and are deposited in great ridges or mounds. Lateral moraines (ma-RAINZ) are those ridges built up along a glacier's sides. A terminal moraine is a mass of debris deposited in front of a glacier, while mounds left beneath the ice are called ground moraines. As earth is scraped from the surrounding valley walls, it also spills onto the surface of the glacier, as represented by the pebbles and sand embedded in the top of your model.

HIDDEN ICE

Icebergs are large chunks of ice that have broken off the ends of glaciers and fallen into the sea. One of the tallest icebergs ever recorded towered more than 400 feet (122 m) above the ocean's surface. That's 100 feet (30 m) taller than the Statue of Liberty! But it's not the ice above the water that poses the greatest danger to passing ships, it's the ice below—the part of the iceberg that can't be seen. The visible chunk of ice rising out of the sea represents just 10 to 15 percent of the iceberg's total size. Knowing that, imagine how big the rest of the "Statue of Liberty" iceberg must have been!

To make your own mini "iceberg," partially fill a plastic bag with water. Tie it tightly and set it in the freezer overnight. The next day, remove the ice chunk from the bag and float it in a sink, tub, or aquarium tank filled with water.

Notice how just the tip of your model iceberg lies above the water's surface, while the rest hangs below. Icebergs float because when water freezes and turns to ice, it takes up more space, becoming less dense, or lighter, than water.

LEARN MORE ABOUT GLACIERS

Glacier
(Internet resource for information
on Antarctica)
http://www.glacier.rice.edu

Glacier National Park
Park Headquarters
West Glacier, MT 59936
http://www.nps.gov/glacier

Glacier Power
(Web site devoted to
glaciological study)
http://www.asf.alaska.edu:2222

Greenland Tourism
Information Office
P.O. Box 1139
DK-1010 Copenhagen
Denmark
http://www.greenland-guide.gl

NASA's Multimedia History of Glacier Bay
(Online journey to Glacier Bay, Alaska)
http://sdcd.gsfc.nasa.gov/glacier.bay/
glacierbay.story.html

National Snow & Ice Data Center (NSIDC)
449 UCB, University of Colorado
Boulder, CO 80309
http://nsidc.org

INDEX

Beautiful and imposing, glaciers are one of Earth's many treasures.